W9-CUX-333

Great African-Americans

Frederick
DOUGLASS

by Isabel Martin   Consulting Editor: Gail Saunders-Smith, PhD

CAPSTONE PRESS
a capstone imprint

Pebble Books are published by Capstone Press,
1710 Roe Crest Drive, North Mankato, Minnesota 56003
www.capstonepub.com

Library of Congress Cataloging-in-Publication Data
Martin, Isabel, 1977–
　Frederick Douglass / by Isabel Martin.
　　pages cm. — (Pebble books. Great African-Americans)
　Includes bibliographical references and index.
　Summary: "Simple text and photographs present the life and achievements
　of Frederick Douglass, a former slave and human rights leader before,
　during, and after the Civil War"—Provided by publisher.
　ISBN 978-1-4914-0501-7 (library binding) — ISBN 978-1-4914-0507-9 (pbk.) —
　ISBN 978-1-4914-0513-0 (ebook pdf)
　1.　Douglass, Frederick, 1818–1895–Juvenile literature. 2.　Slaves–United States–
Biography–Juvenile literature. 3.　Abolitionists–United States–Biography–Juvenile
literature. 4.　African American abolitionists–Biography–Juvenile literature. 5.　Antislavery
movements–United States–History–Juvenile literature. 6.　African Americans–History–19th
century–Juvenile literature.　I. Title.
　E449.D75C368 2015
　973.8092–dc23
　[B]　　　　　　　　　　　　　　　2013049777

Editorial Credits
Nikki Bruno Clapper, editor; Terri Poburka, designer; Kelly Garvin, media researcher;
Laura Manthe, production specialist

Photo Credits
Alamy Images: Everett Collection Historical, 14; North Wind Picture Archive, 16; Corbis/
Bettmann, 12; Getty Images, Inc.: Hulton Archive, 4, Stock Montage, cover; The Granger
Collection, 8; Library of Congress, 20; The George F. Landegger Collection of DC,
Photographs in Carol M. Highsmith's America, 18; Moorland-Spingarn Research Center,
Howard University, 10; North Wind Picture Archive, 6; Shutterstock/Eliks, cover art

Note to Parents and Teachers

The Great African-Americans set supports national curriculum standards for social
studies related to people, places, and environments. This book describes and illustrates
Frederick Douglass. The images support early readers in understanding the text. The
repetition of words and phrases helps early readers learn new words. This book also
introduces early readers to subject-specific vocabulary words, which are defined in the
Glossary section. Early readers may need assistance to read some words and to use the
Table of Contents, Glossary, Read More, Internet Sites, and Index sections of the book.

Printed in the United States of America in Stevens Point, Wisconsin.
032014　　　008092WZF14

Table of Contents

Early Life

Frederick Douglass
was born around 1818
in Maryland. He was a
famous writer and speaker.
He fought against slavery.
People all over the world
respected him.

a slave cabin

AROUND
1818
born

1825
goes to work
for owner

Frederick and his family were slaves. His owners took him away from his mother. His grandmother cared for him until 1825. Then he had to work in his owner's house.

young Frederick learning to read

AROUND **1818**
born

1825
goes to work for owner

1826
moves to Baltimore

In 1826 Frederick
was sent to a new
owner in Baltimore.
Frederick learned to read.
He read that some slaves
escaped to freedom.
He wanted to be free.

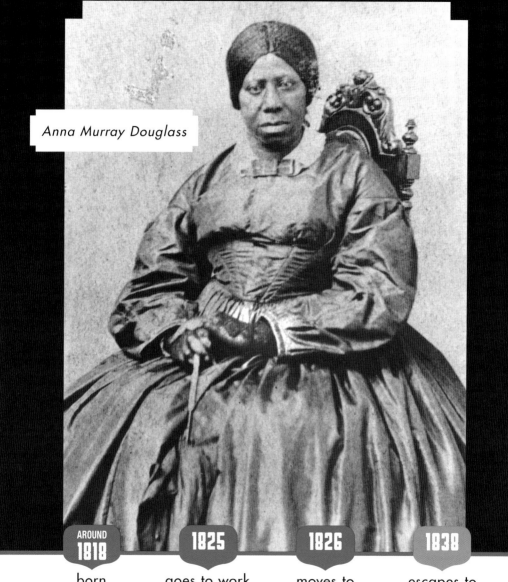

Anna Murray Douglass

AROUND
1818
born

1825
goes to work
for owner

1826
moves to
Baltimore

1838
escapes to
New York

A Free Young Adult

Frederick met a free black woman named Anna Murray. In 1838 Anna helped Frederick escape. They went to New York. Frederick and Anna got married.

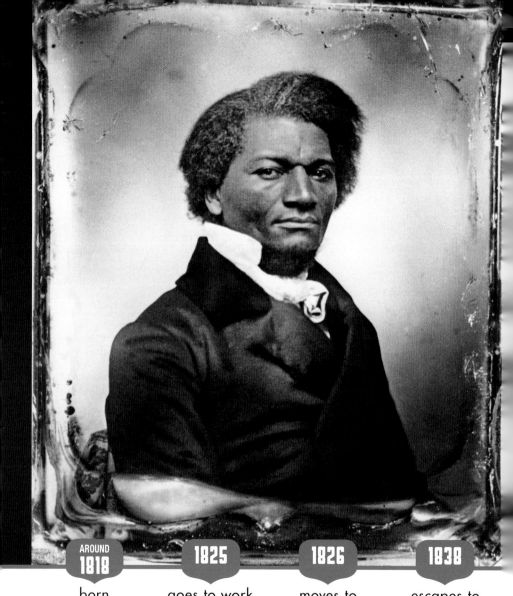

AROUND 1818	1825	1826	1838
born	goes to work for owner	moves to Baltimore	escapes to New York

Frederick did not want
his old owner to find him.
It was against the law
for slaves to escape.
So he changed his last
name to Douglass.

Frederick speaking at an abolitionist meeting

AROUND 1818	1825	1826	1838
born	goes to work for owner	moves to Baltimore	escapes to New York

Middle Years

In 1841 Frederick went to his first abolitionist meeting. Abolitionists worked to end slavery. Frederick gave speeches at many meetings. He said slavery was wrong.

1841

goes to first
abolitionist meeting

Frederick speaking about slavery in England

AROUND 1818	1825	1826	1838
born	goes to work for owner	moves to Baltimore	escapes to New York

In 1845 Frederick wrote
a book about his life.
He went to England and
spoke about slavery.
In 1846 two Englishmen
bought Frederick's freedom
from his old owner.

1841
goes to first
abolitionist meeting

1845
writes book
about his life

1846
gets freed
from old owner

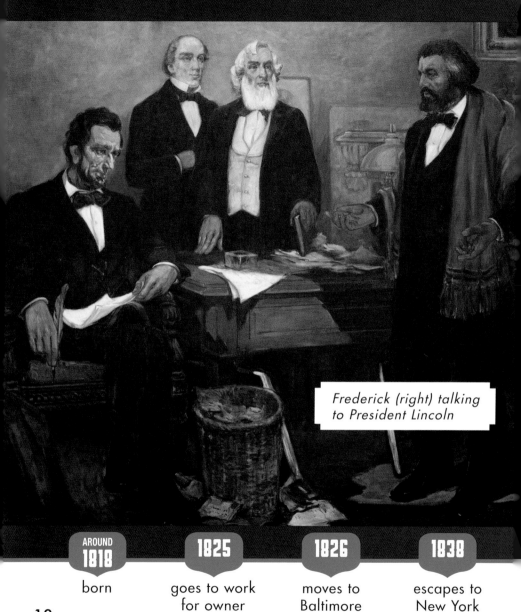

Frederick (right) talking to President Lincoln

AROUND 1818	1825	1826	1838
born	goes to work for owner	moves to Baltimore	escapes to New York

In 1861 the Civil War started. The North and the South fought about slavery. Two of Frederick's sons were soldiers for the North. Frederick asked President Lincoln to end slavery.

1841	**1845**	**1846**
goes to first abolitionist meeting	writes book about his life	gets freed from old owner

Frederick lived in this house
from 1877 until his death.

AROUND 1818	1825	1826	1838
born	goes to work for owner	moves to Baltimore	escapes to New York

Later in Life

In 1865 the Civil War ended.
American slaves were freed.
Later, Frederick held important
government jobs. He died in
1895. People remember him
as a freedom fighter.

1841	1845	1846	1895
goes to first abolitionist meeting	writes book about his life	gets freed from old owner	dies

Glossary

abolitionist—a person who worked to end slavery

Civil War (1861–1865)—the battle between states in the North and South that led to the end of slavery in the United States

escape—to get away from

freedom—the right to live the way you want

government—the group of people who make laws, rules, and decisions for a country or state

respect—to believe in the quality and worth of others and yourself

slave—a person who is owned by another person

slavery—the owning of other people; slaves are forced to work without pay.

soldier—a person who is in the military

Read More

Cline-Ransome, Lesa. *Words Set Me Free: The Story of Young Frederick Douglass.* New York: Simon & Schuster Books for Young Readers, 2012.

Kalman, Maira. *Looking at Lincoln.* New York: Nancy Paulsen Books, 2012.

Slade, Suzanne. *Friends for Freedom: The Story of Susan B. Anthony & Frederick Douglass.* Watertown, Mass.: Charlesbridge, 2014.

Internet Sites

FactHound offers a safe, fun way to find Internet sites related to this book. All of the sites on FactHound have been researched by our staff.

Here's all you do:
Visit *www.facthound.com*
Type in this code: 9781491405017

Check out projects, games and lots more at
www.capstonekids.com

Critical Thinking Using the Common Core

1. Why do you think lots of people respected Frederick? (Key Ideas and Details)

2. What kinds of information can you find in the chapter called "A Free Young Adult"? (Craft and Structure)

Index

Word Count: 246
Grade: 1
Early-Intervention Level: 20